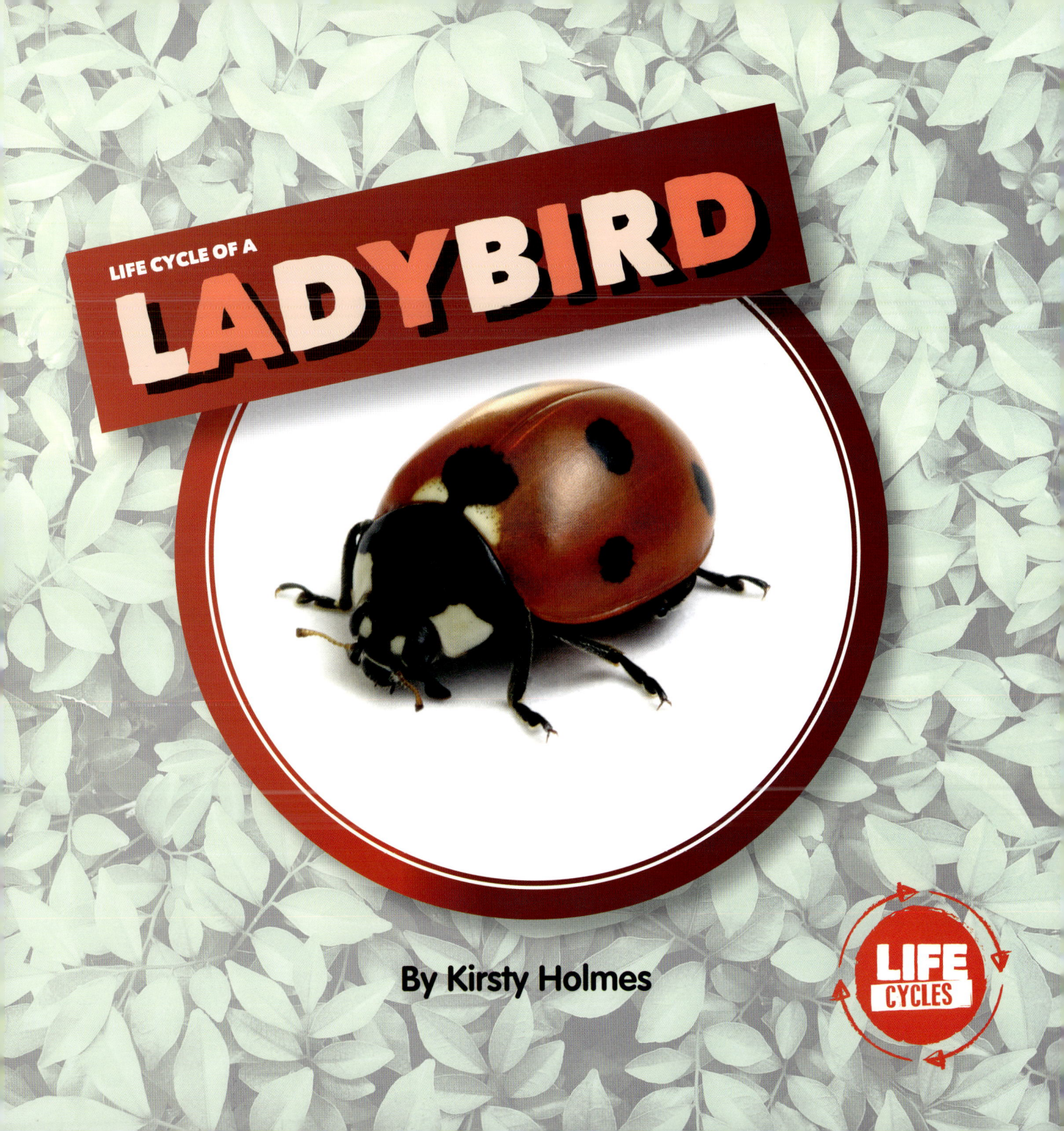

Words that look like **this** can be found in the glossary on page 24.

©2020
BookLife Publishing Ltd.
King's Lynn
Norfolk PE30 4LS

ISBN: 978-1-78637-936-8

All rights reserved. Printed in Malaysia.

All facts, statistics, web addresses and URLs in this book were verified as valid and accurate at time of writing. No responsibility for any changes to external websites or references can be accepted by either the author or publisher.

Written by:
Kirsty Holmes

Edited by:
Robin Twiddy

Designed by:
Brandon Mattless

A catalogue record for this book is available from the British Library.

PHOTO CREDITS

All images are courtesy of shutterstock.com, unless otherwise specified. With thanks to Getty Images, Thinkstock Photo and iStockphoto. Front Cover & 1 – pernsanitzfoto, irin-k. 2 – Leonid Ikan. 3 – KKphotographer, Mks.G.A, Christiane Godin. 4 – GSK919, StockImageFactory.com. 5 – India Picture, michaeljung, StockImageFactory.com. 6 – Antonio Gravante. 7 – AdaCo. 8 – Brett Hondow. 9 – KKphotographer, schankz. 10 – Henri Koskinen. 11 – thatmacroguy. 12 – ozgur kerem bulur. 13 – matunka. 14 – JonRichfield. 15 – Protasov AN. 16 – Mks.G.A, JFCerez. 17 – Rachasie. 18 – LedyX, lewalp, aaltair. 19 – vitek3ds, max dallocco, TungCheung, DenisNata. 20 – Wattlebird. 21 – Christiane Godin. 22 – mchin, Anest, Gilles San Martin. 23 – Young Swee Ming, Henri Koskinen, Ger Bosma Photos.

LIFE CYCLE OF A LADYBIRD

Page 4	**What Is a Life Cycle?**
Page 6	**Lovely Ladybirds**
Page 8	**Excellent Eggs**
Page 10	**Loads of Larvae**
Page 12	**Perfect Pupae**
Page 14	**Loopy Ladybirds**
Page 16	**Life as a Ladybird**
Page 18	**Fun Facts about Ladybirds**
Page 20	**The End of Life as a Ladybird**
Page 22	**The Life Cycle**
Page 24	**Glossary and Index**

WHAT IS A LIFE CYCLE?

All living things have a life cycle. They are all born, they all grow bigger, and their bodies change.

When they are fully grown, they have **offspring** of their own. In the end, all living things die. This is the life cycle.

LOVELY LADYBIRDS

A ladybird is a type of beetle. This means it is an insect, with six legs and hard front wings. These wings are not used for flying. They cover and protect a soft pair of wings underneath.

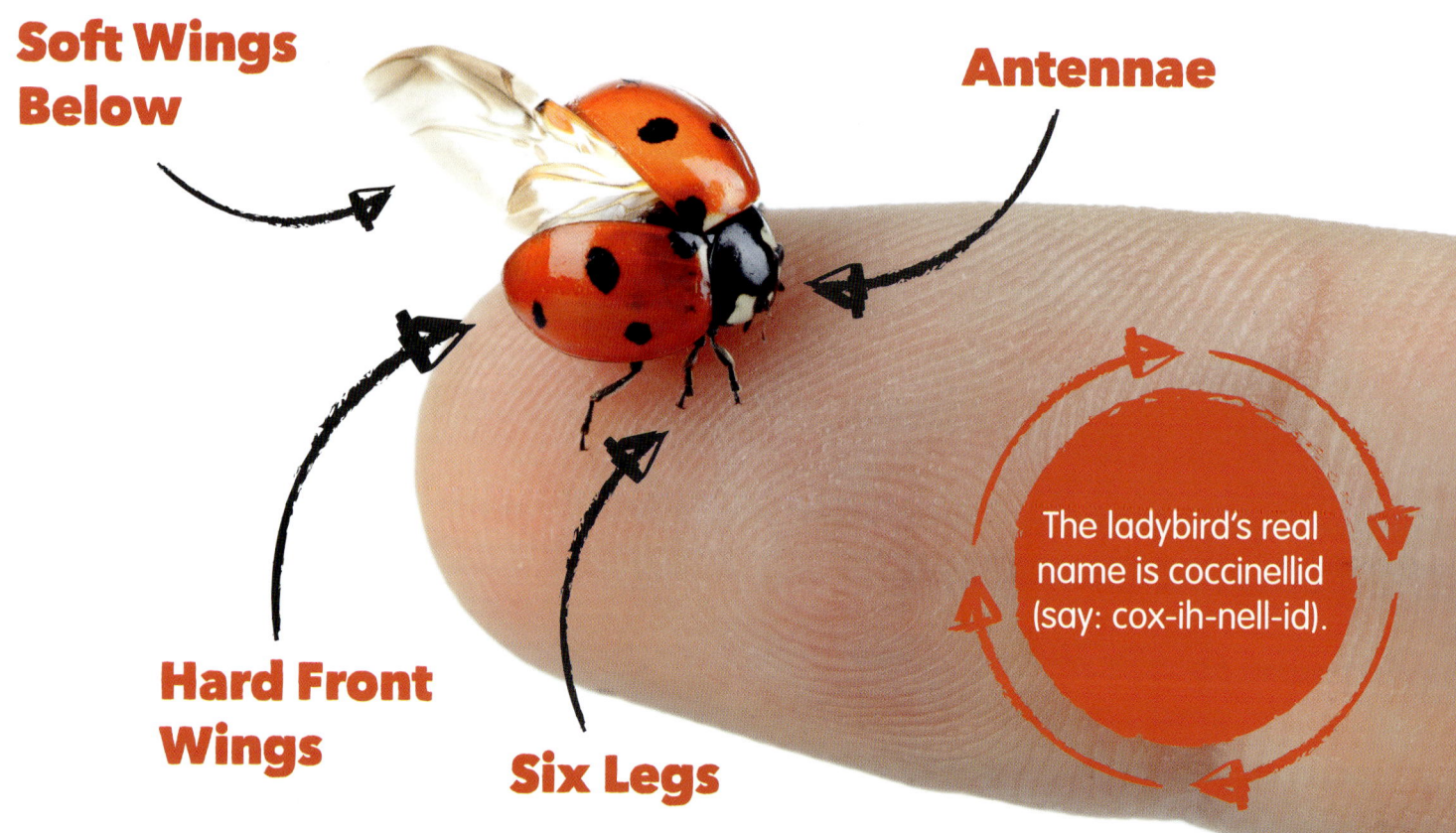

Soft Wings Below

Antennae

Hard Front Wings

Six Legs

The ladybird's real name is coccinellid (say: cox-ih-nell-id).

Can you spot the ladybird?

Ladybirds are often red with black spots, but they can also come in other bright patterns. These bright colours scare off **predators**. Ladybirds are very small. The largest they can grow to is around ten millimetres.

EXCELLENT EGGS

Female Ladybird Laying Eggs

In the summer months, a female ladybird can lay around 1,000 eggs. The female lays her eggs in groups, usually on the underside of a leaf. The eggs are orange or yellow.

The female ladybird will often lay her eggs close to a **colony** of aphids. Aphids are small insects with soft bodies. They drink the **sap** of plants. They are also a ladybird's favourite food!

Aphid

LOADS OF LARVAE

After four to ten days, the eggs hatch. The **larvae** come out of the eggs, but they don't look like ladybirds yet. Larvae may be black, brown or grey, and they may have yellow and orange patches.

Larva

This larva has **shed** its skin. Can you see the larva and the old skin?

The larvae are very hungry and will eat lots of aphids. As the larvae grow, they get too big for their skins. They grow a new one underneath, then shed the old skin.

PERFECT PUPAE

When the larvae have shed their skins for the last time, they find a leaf to attach themselves to. They don't move or eat. They change from larvae to **pupae.**

Pupae stay still for up to two weeks. Inside, the bodies of the larvae are changing. They are making their wings and legs, ready to become adults.

LOOPY LADYBIRDS

The adult ladybird will be pale and soft when it comes out. As it dries, its outer wings will harden. The ladybird will get its colour now, too.

This newly hatched adult is drying in the sun.

Ladybirds come in different colours, and each **species** has its own pattern. Most ladybirds are red, black, orange or yellow. Many ladybird species have spots, but some have stripes instead.

LIFE AS A LADYBIRD

Adult ladybirds look for food. They are **omnivores** and they like to eat aphids, whiteflies and mealybugs. Some species like to eat caterpillars. They also eat plants, pollen, nectar and **fungi**.

Mealybug

This ladybird lives in a rice field.

Rice

Aphids eat plants and **crops**. Gardeners and farmers like ladybirds to live in their gardens because ladybirds eat aphids. Ladybirds can eat up to 50 aphids each day. This keeps the plants and crops safe.

FUN FACTS ABOUT LADYBIRDS

- Ladybirds are also known as ladybugs and lady beetles.

- There are over 6,000 different types of ladybird in the world.

- The ladybird spider has a red **abdomen** and looks a bit like a ladybird. It lives in Dorset in the UK.

- Ladybirds smell through their antennae and their feet!

Ladybirds live on every continent except Antarctica.

THE END OF LIFE AS A LADYBIRD

These ladybirds are **hibernating** underneath this light.

Most ladybirds live for around one year. In the winter, they gather together in a group. This helps them keep warm. Most will die, but the ones that live will **mate** again in the spring.

Many predators like to eat ladybirds. Toads catch them on their long, sticky tongues, spiders trap them in their webs and birds catch them in the air.

This spider has caught a tasty lunch.

THE LIFE CYCLE

The egg hatches into a larva. This becomes a pupa and changes into an adult ladybird.

The adult goes on to have offspring of its own.

23

GLOSSARY

abdomen	the rear section of an insect's body
colony	a group of animals living in one place
crops	plants that are grown on a large scale to be eaten or used
fungi	living things that look like plants but have no flowers
hibernating	spending the winter sleeping or in a dormant state to save energy
larvae	young animals that must grow and change form before they become adults
mate	to produce young with an animal of the same species
offspring	the young of an animal or plant
omnivores	animals that eat both plants and other animals
predators	animals that hunt other animals for food
pupae	insects at the stage of change between larvae and adult
sap	a sweet liquid found in plants
shed	to remove and replace the skin or shell with another one that has grown underneath
species	a group of very similar animals or plants that can create young together

INDEX

aphids 9, 11, 16-17
eggs 8-10, 22
feet 19
ladybird spiders 18
larvae 10-13, 22
predators 7, 21
pupae 12-13, 22-23
spots 7, 15
wings 6, 13-14